GOBLIN
LIFE CYCLES

by Noah Leatherland

Minneapolis, Minnesota

Credits
All images courtesy of Shutterstock.com. With thanks to Adobe Stock, Getty Images, Thinkstock Photo, and iStockphoto. Cover – Luca Lorenzelli, Sergio Photone, Here, Jakub Krechowicz, sociologas, wabeno. Recurring – Elizaveta Mironets, sociologas, wabeno. P1 – Luca Lorenzelli. P4–5 – JGade, elebeZoom. P6–7 – tsuneomp, Joeprachatree. P8–9 – Henk, nobeastsofierce, Gustavo Tabosa. P10–11 – xpixel, KYNA STUDIO, Katrina Bianchi. P12–13 – Holiday.Photo.Top, PixelSquid3d, tsuneomp, SmileStudio. P14–15 – Sport08, NisanatStudio, Steve Collender, asadykov. P16–17 – Sport08, Matthew Troke. P18–19 – AKaiser, Wachiwit, ismail albayrak, DomCritelli, Holiday.Photo.Top. P20–21 – Philll, Garno Studio, tsuneomp, Oleksandr Khoma. P22–23 – Declan Hillman, DM7. P24–25 – Natalie Board, Pixel-Shot, xpixel. P26–27 – Benedek Alpar, RJ22, New Africa, Adam Radosavljevic, LightField Studios. P28–29 – antpkr, tsuneomp. P30 – OP38Studio.

Bearport Publishing Company Product Development Team
President: Jen Jenson; Director of Product Development: Spencer Brinker; Managing Editor: Allison Juda; Associate Editor: Naomi Reich; Associate Editor: Tiana Tran; Art Director: Colin O'Dea; Designer: Kim Jones; Designer: Kayla Eggert; Product Development Assistant: Owen Hamlin

Library of Congress Cataloging-in-Publication Data

Names: Leatherland, Noah, 1999- author.
Title: Goblin life cycles / by Noah Leatherland.
Description: Roar! books. | Minneapolis, Minnesota : Bearport Publishing
  Company, [2025] | Series: Paranormal life cycles | Includes
  bibliographical references and index.
Identifiers: LCCN 2024010956 (print) | LCCN 2024010957 (ebook) | ISBN
  9798892320566 (library binding) | ISBN 9798892325301 (paperback) | ISBN
  9798892321891 (ebook)
Subjects: LCSH: Goblins--Juvenile literature. | Life cycles
  (Biology)--Juvenile literature.
Classification: LCC GR549 .L38 2025 (print) | LCC GR549 (ebook) | DDC
  398.24/54--dc23/eng/20240307
LC record available at https://lccn.loc.gov/2024010956
LC ebook record available at https://lccn.loc.gov/2024010957

© 2025 BookLife Publishing
This edition is published by arrangement with BookLife Publishing.

North American adaptations © 2025 Bearport Publishing Company. All rights reserved. No part of this publication may be reproduced in whole or in part, stored in any retrieval system, or transmitted in any form or by any means, electronic, mechanical, photocopying, recording, or otherwise, without written permission from the publisher. Bearport Publishing is a division of Chrysalis Education Group.

For more information, write to Bearport Publishing, 5357 Penn Avenue South, Minneapolis, MN 55419.

CONTENTS

WHAT IS A LIFE CYCLE? 4
WHAT IS A GOBLIN? 6
MAKING A GOBLIN 8
THE EARLY GOBLIN 10
GROWING FROM GOO 12
DIET 14
HABITAT 16
THE OLD GOBLIN 18
GROWING NEW GOBLINS 20
TYPES OF GOBLINS 22
SPOTTING A GOBLIN 24
HOW TO DEAL WITH A GOBLIN 26
LIFE CYCLE OF A GOBLIN 28
BEWARE THE PARANORMAL! 30
GLOSSARY 31
INDEX 32
READ MORE 32
LEARN MORE ONLINE 32

WHAT IS A LIFE CYCLE?

Every living thing has a life cycle. Over this cycle, living things grow and change.

Eventually, they die. Living things **reproduce** so the cycle carries on after they are gone. This is all a normal part of living.

But what about the world of **legendary** creatures? Surely **paranormal** beings would have a beginning, middle, and end to life, too.

People often explain things they don't understand by telling stories. Sometimes, the stories have very strange creatures!

What would a goblin life cycle be like? Let's imagine. . . .

WHAT IS A GOBLIN?

Myths about goblins tell of mean, evil creatures. Goblins have different names in different **cultures**. But almost all goblins are said to make a mess wherever they go.

These paranormal beings are either **invisible** or very good at hiding.

Some British myths call goblins redcaps. In Germany, there are stories about kobold goblins.

Goblins are said to look a little humanlike but are usually smaller than people. They have sharp teeth and claws.

Many stories describe goblins as having a green color. They are often dirty and maybe even slimy.

MAKING A GOBLIN

Since they are so nasty, goblins probably wouldn't have a normal start to life. Maybe goblins start as **spores**.

Some mosses, ferns, and **algae** reproduce with spores. They send out these tiny seedlike parts to make more of themselves.

Ferns

Spores

Spores usually settle in places that are damp. A human nose might be just right for goblin spores! There, they could mix with snot to get nice and gross.

Once they are ready for the next step of the life cycle, the goblin spores could spread far and wide when we sneeze them out.

Sneezes spread germs. Cover your mouth and nose when you sneeze . . . even if you don't believe in goblins!

THE EARLY GOBLIN

After the snotty spores have settled, goblins would probably become a goo. This is sort of what happens to some kinds of algae that reproduce using spores. Lumps of the green goblin gunk would spring up all around where the spores landed.

Goblin gunk would probably be very sticky. It may be able to stick itself to the floor, walls, and even the ceiling.

Goblin gunk?

Algae on a pond

A slimy coating helps algae stay safe.

Some of the gunk might start to change. It could harden and reshape into the body of a goblin.

You can imagine the slimy pile begin to bubble as the goblin grows. You might even start to hear the baby goblin squealing.

GROWING FROM GOO

What would happen during the next part of the goblin's life cycle? The goblin might have to get out of the goo pile. A goblin is supposed to have claws. It could use them to slice its way out of the gunk.

Animals use their claws to fight off enemies, dig, climb, and even groom themselves.

Young goblins would probably be very small. Many animals start out as smaller versions of their adult selves.

In order to grow, most creatures need to eat. That would be the next thing for a goblin to do.

DIET

A goblin's sharp teeth would be able to rip almost anything into tiny pieces.

However, if they were small, young goblins probably couldn't hunt. So, the creatures would likely eat whatever they could get their hands on. What have you left on the floor?

Old toenails, lost coins, and forgotten hair ties could be part of a goblin's diet. So could crumbs or any trash we toss.

Have you ever lost one of the socks from a pair? Maybe the other one became a goblin snack!

Many pests, including rodents and bugs, are drawn to crumbs and food scraps.

Goblin food?

HABITAT

You've probably never seen a goblin. If they existed, goblins would live in tucked-away corners where they couldn't be found. Their eyes would need to be good at seeing in a **habitat** with little light.

Living outside would be dangerous for goblins because there are a lot of **predators** that could eat them. This may explain why legends say goblins live inside human homes.

Goblins could settle under sinks, behind fridges, inside toilets, or in basements.

They would need to stay hidden by coming out to look for food only during the night. If they ate enough, goblins would grow.

Animals that are mostly active at night are called nocturnal.

THE OLD GOBLIN

What would happen as goblins grow into adults? Like with humans, a goblin's hair might turn white. Perhaps this would happen to hair on their heads. Or maybe the white hair grows out of their ears and noses.

In some stories, a goblin's claws never stop growing. That would mean old goblins would have very long claws.

The spots hair grows out of make less color as they age. That's why our hair turns white as we get older.

For the life cycle to continue, goblins would need to have young. That might mean you could find goblin goo in your basement or crawl space. But where would the gunk come from?

If you spot something slimy around your home, don't touch it. Tell an adult right away!

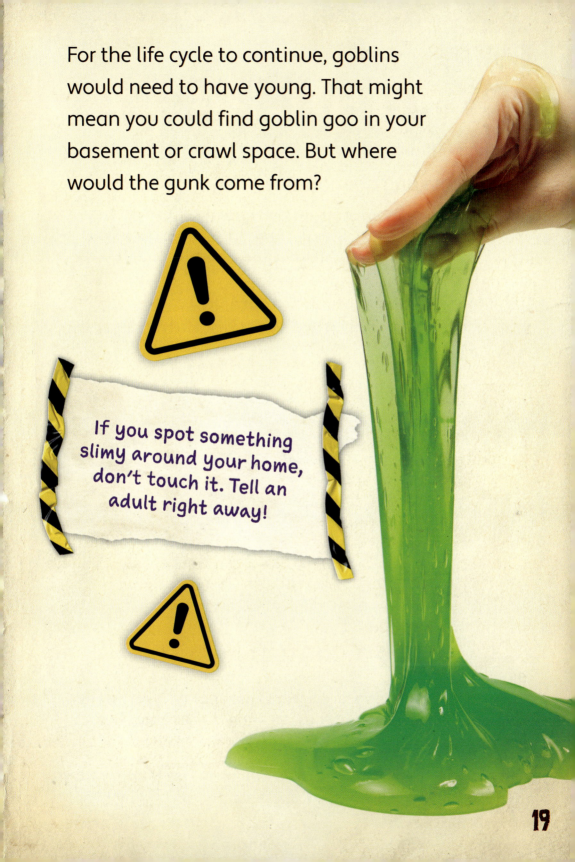

GROWING NEW GOBLINS

Most plants and animals need to get big and strong before they make healthy new life.

To make more spores, a goblin would probably need to eat as much as possible. They'd probably stuff themselves until they were about to burst!

Praying mantis mothers eat their partners to get energy just before laying eggs.

A goblin would then need to let out spores to start the cycle again. Of course, they would probably do it in a really gross way. Maybe spores would come out of tiny holes all over the goblin's back.

Goblin spores?

These spores could end up in people's noses. With more snotty spores, the goblin's life cycle could carry on even after a goblin gets old and dies.

TYPES OF GOBLINS

There are many stories of different kinds of goblins.

EVIL GOBLINS

Some goblins are only supposed to cause **mischief**. Others are truly evil. What could make them so bad?

Maybe the worst goblins are sneezed out by very mean people.

Some of the friendly goblins in stories are called hobgoblins.

MUCK GOBLINS

Muck goblins are extra gross. They are nasty, even for goblins. Maybe they come out of the noses of people with colds. The sick snot could make the spores thicker and heavier.

That would probably lead to even slimier goblin gunk. Because of this, muck goblins are thought to be messier than other goblins.

Spotting a Goblin

Where might you look for a goblin? There could be signs all around.

Tissues

Check around you to see if there are any tissues wiggling. If snotty spores make goblins, there might be some goblins growing in snotty tissues.

Used tissues are often covered in germs. Touching them can pass along illnesses.

TRASH CANS

Goblins might get stuck in trash cans while looking for food. Remember, goblins are thought to eat just about anything!

DIRT

Look out for tiny, dirty footprints. Gross goblins would get into all sorts of messes that could stick to the bottoms of their feet.

HOW TO DEAL WITH A
GOBLIN

How could you get rid of a goblin if one got cozy in your home?

AIR FRESHENERS

Goblins live in dark, wet places that could easily start to smell bad. Air fresheners make the air a bit more pleasant. Nice smells could chase goblins away.

TOSS TRASH

Make sure all your trash gets thrown away properly. Any garbage left out could bring in hungry goblins.

Keeping your home clean is one way to keep yourself healthy.

CLEANING

Maybe a vacuum cleaner could suck up goblin spores.

Cleaning sprays and wet wipes would probably work on goblin gunk.

Wash your hands! This could stop spores from getting into your nose.

LIFE CYCLE OF A GOBLIN

So, what might the life cycle of a goblin look like? It may start with goblin spores. These spores could get inside a person's nose.

If that person sneezed, the snotty spores would spread. Then, goblin gunk may start to form. A goblin could grow in the gunk.

The start of a goblin?

Soon, a new goblin would slash its way out using sharp claws. Then, the goblin would eat all sorts of gross things in order to grow.

If it got full enough, the goblin could shoot out more spores. These would spread in the air, and the life cycle could continue.

Almost all living things grow, make young, and die. But some kinds of jellyfish can make themselves young even after dying!

BEWARE THE PARANORMAL!

There are stories around the world of all sorts of paranormal creatures. If you want to learn more, be very careful. . . .

Goblins may be gross, but what if there is something even worse creeping around in the dark? How would their scary life cycle begin, continue, and end?

GLOSSARY

algae tiny plantlike living things that grow in water

cultures the customs and traditions shared by groups of people

habitat a place in nature where a plant or animal normally lives

invisible unable to be seen

legendary related to stories handed down from long ago that are often based on some facts but cannot be proven true

mischief playful behavior that may cause trouble

myths old stories that tell of strange or magical events and creatures

nocturnal active at night

paranormal events that are not able to be scientifically explained

predators animals that hunt and kill other animals for food

reproduce to make more of a living thing

spores tiny structures that are made by living things that can become new individuals of that life form

INDEX

claws 7, 12, 18, 29
cleaning 26–27
diet 14–15
dirt 25
goblin gunk 10–12, 19, 23, 27–28
habitat 16
hobgoblins 22
life cycle 4–5, 9, 12, 19, 21, 28–30
muck goblins 23
paranormal 5–6, 30
snot 9–10, 21, 23–24, 28
spores 8–10, 20–21, 23–24, 27–29
teeth 7, 14
trash 15, 25–26

READ MORE

Gieseke, Tyler. *Plant and Animal Life Cycles (Earth Cycles).* Minneapolis: Pop!, 2023.

Owen, Ruth. *Reproduction (Biology Basics: Need to Know).* Minneapolis: Bearport Publishing Company, 2024.

LEARN MORE ONLINE

1. Go to **www.factsurfer.com** or scan the QR code below.

2. Enter **"Goblin Life Cycle"** into the search box.

3. Click on the cover of this book to see a list of websites.